THIS COLORING BOOK

BELONG TO:

____

____

COUNT VAMPY

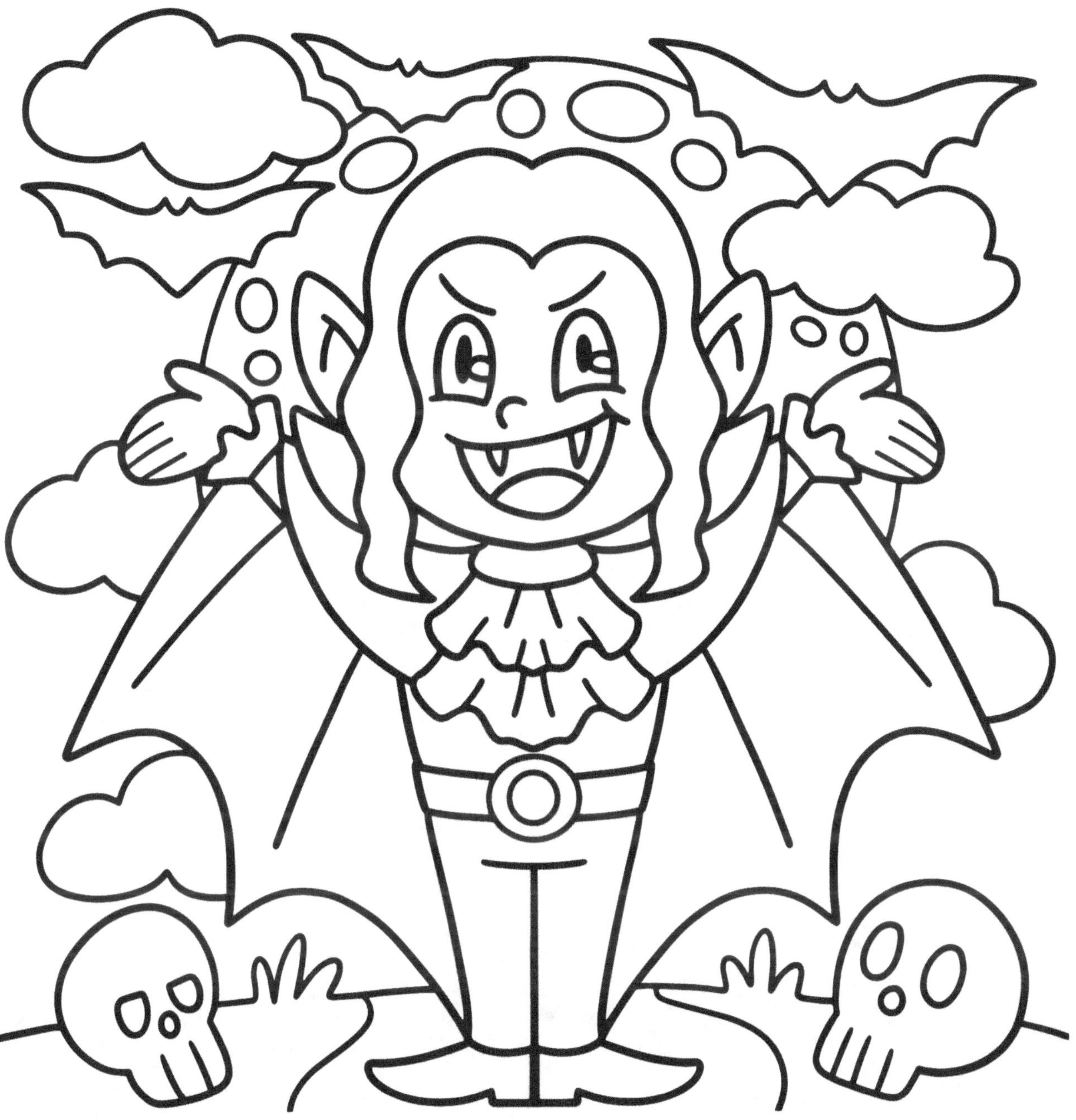

Meet Count Vampy, the friendly vampire who loves to dance under the moonlight!

ZIPPY ZOMBIE

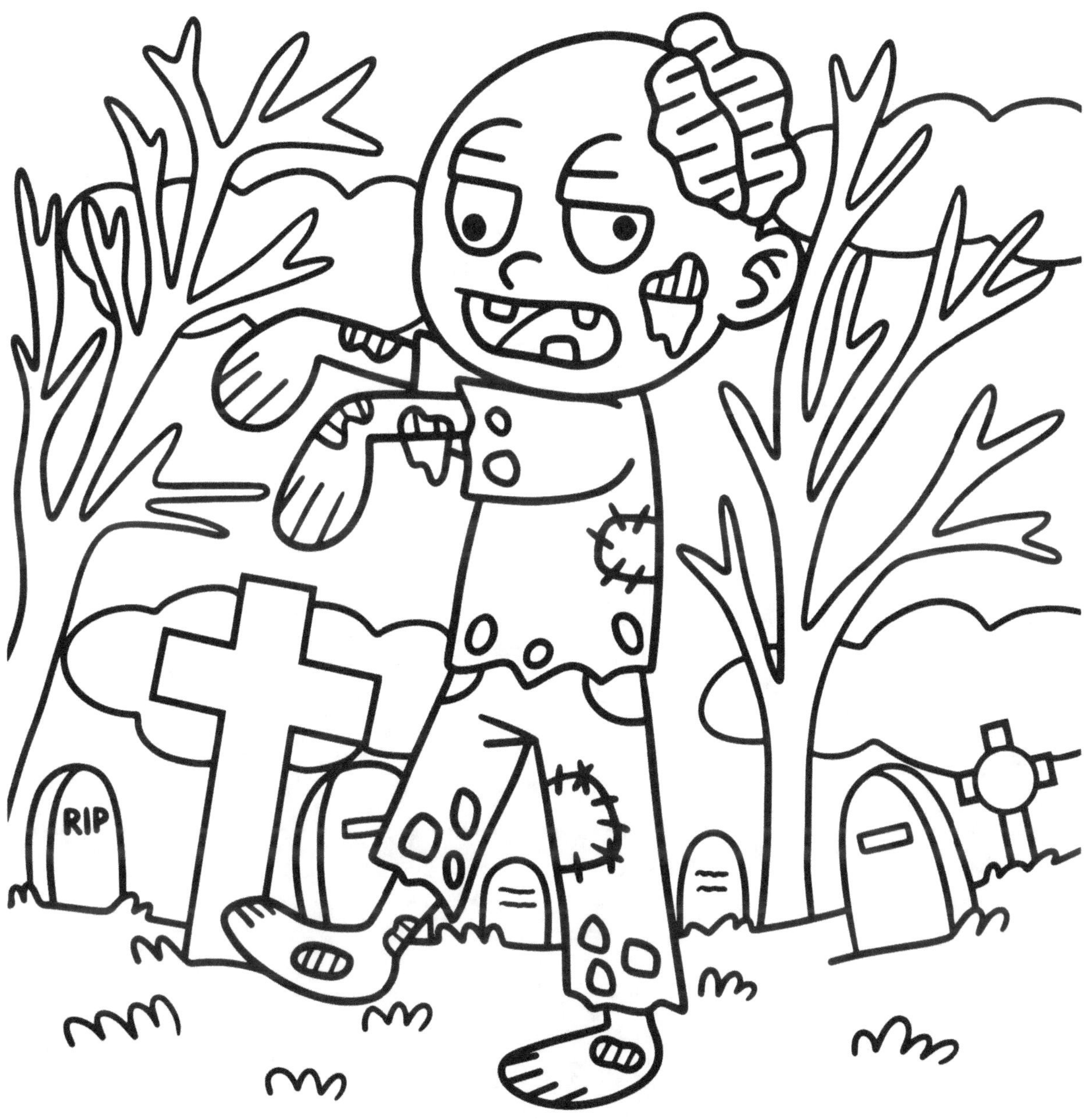

This is Zippy the zombie. a silly creature who loves to shuffle and groan all day long!

FRANKY THE MONSTER

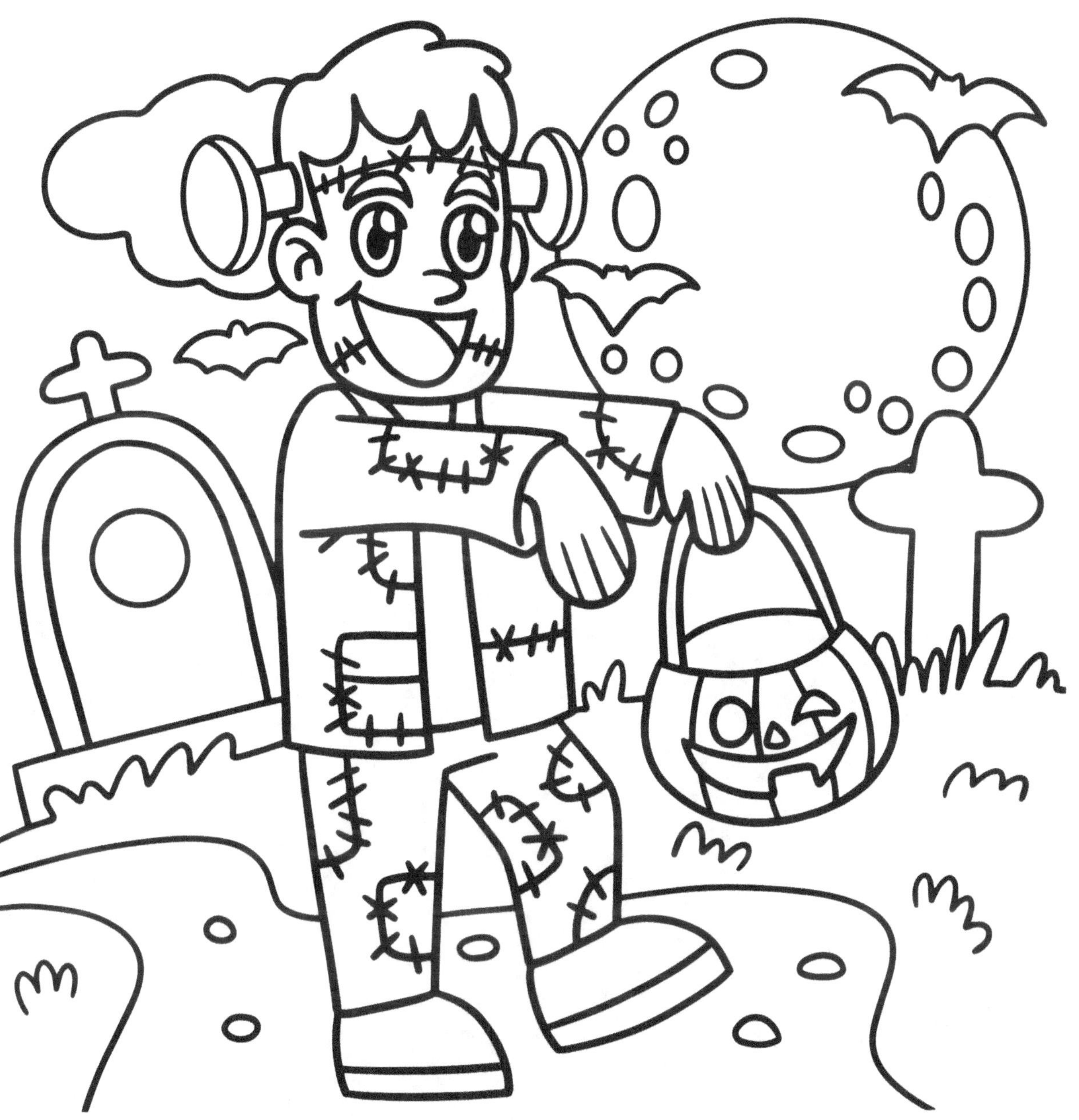

Say hello to Franky the Monster, a friendly creature with big fuzzy arms and a goofy smile!

LISA THE MUMMY

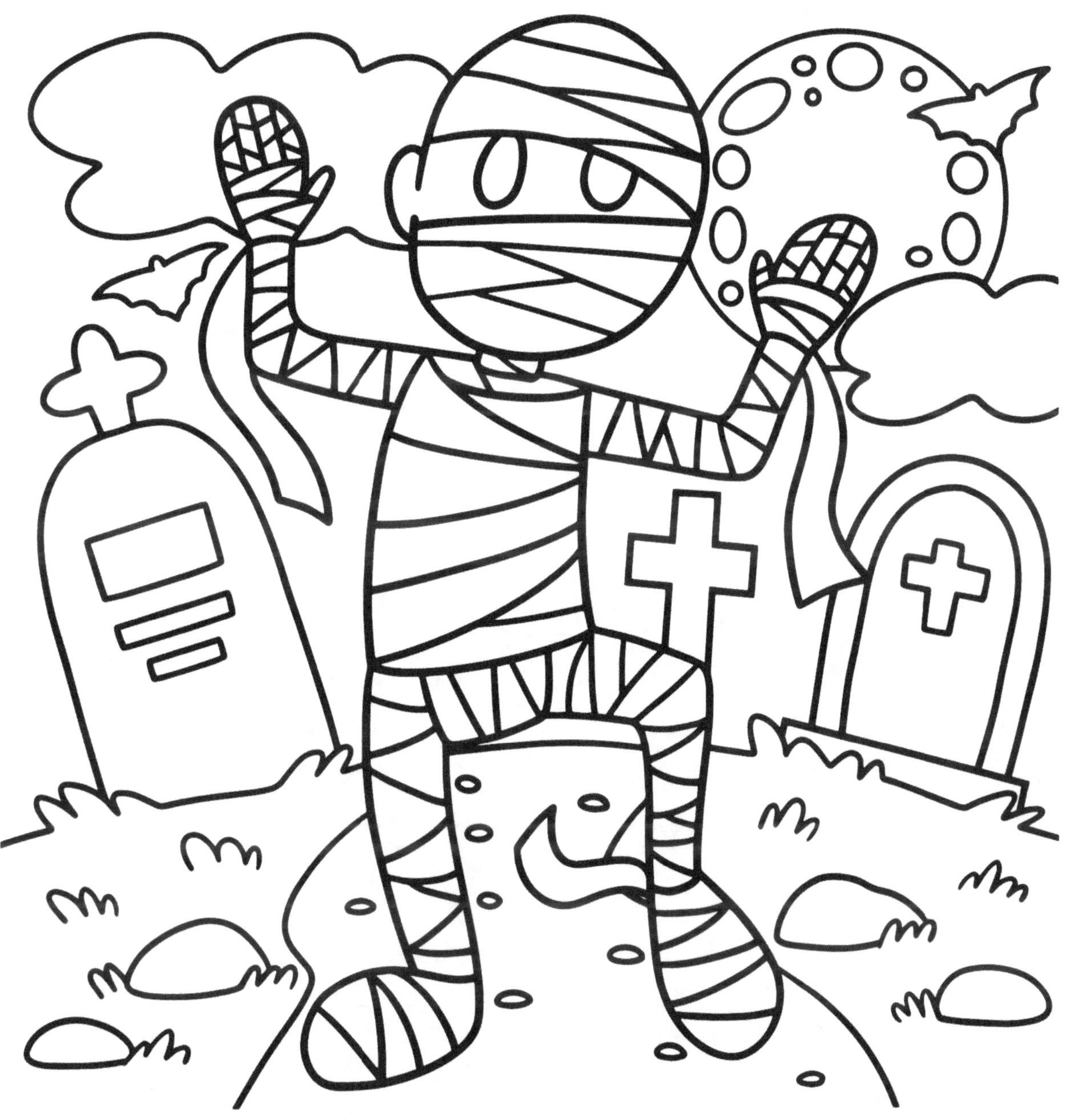

Meet Lisa the Mummy, a wrapped-up wonder with eyes that sparkle and secrets to uncover.

MAX THE WOLF

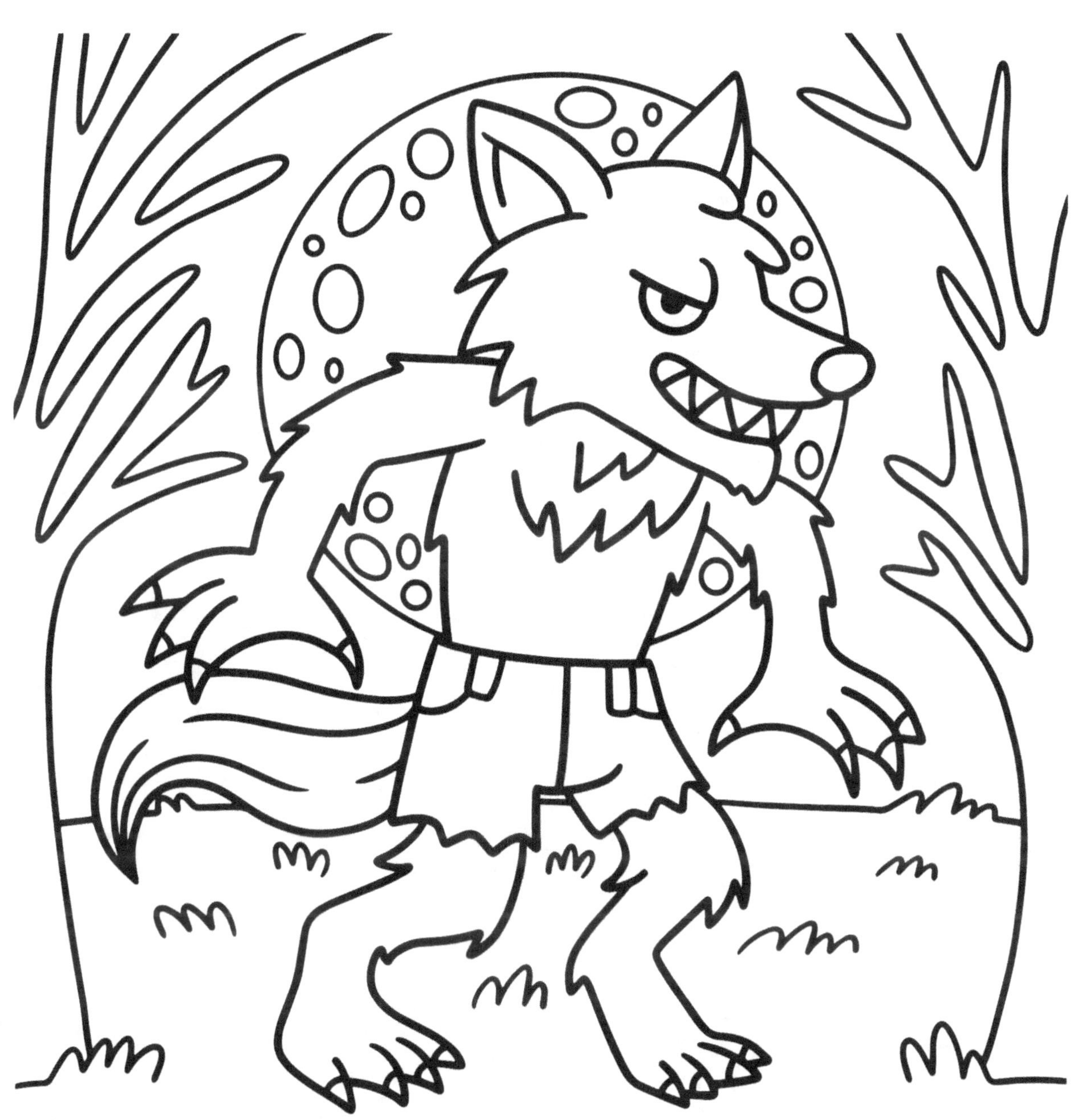

Watch out for this silly wolf, with a big grin and a wagging tail, let's give it some colorful flair, and make it howl with joy and wail!

SARAH THE WITCH

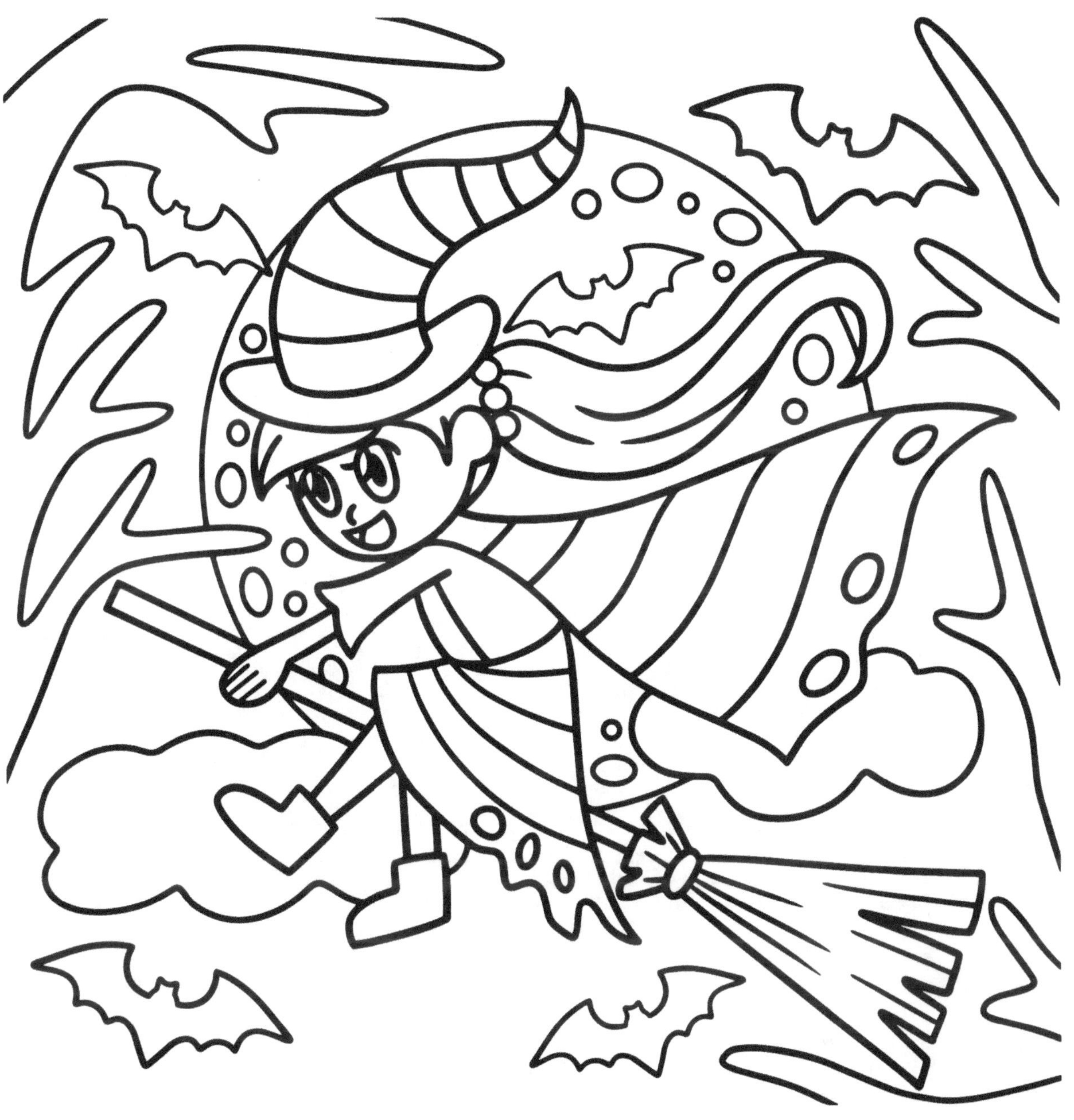

Fly on your broom, cast spells with glee, this witch in the picture is full of glee! Grab your colors and make her shine!

PIGGY BAT

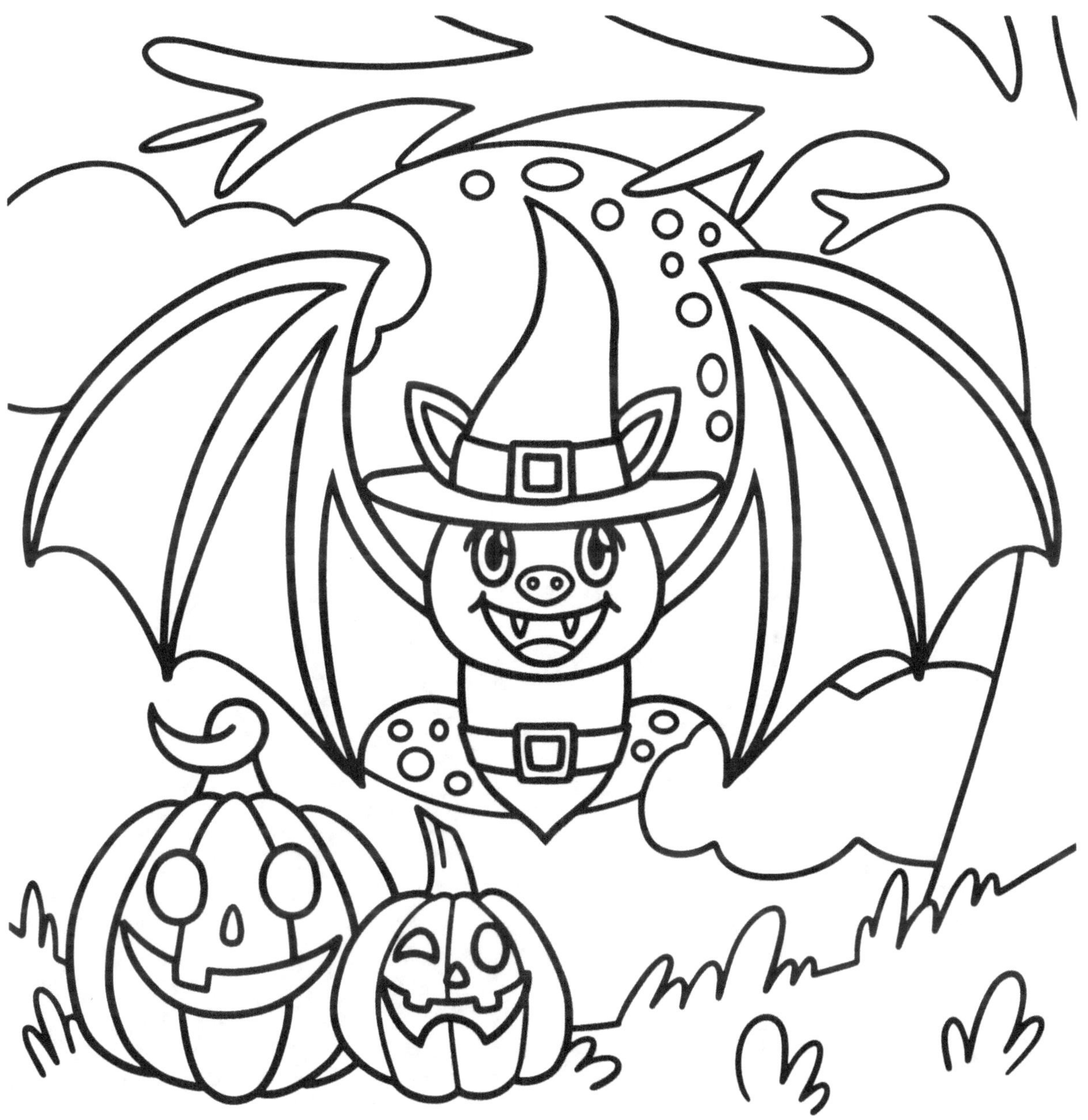

Meet the pigbat! It's a magical creature that looks like a pig with wings. Imagine a cute little piggy flying in the sky. Say hello to the pigbat and let your imagination take flight!

GHOST

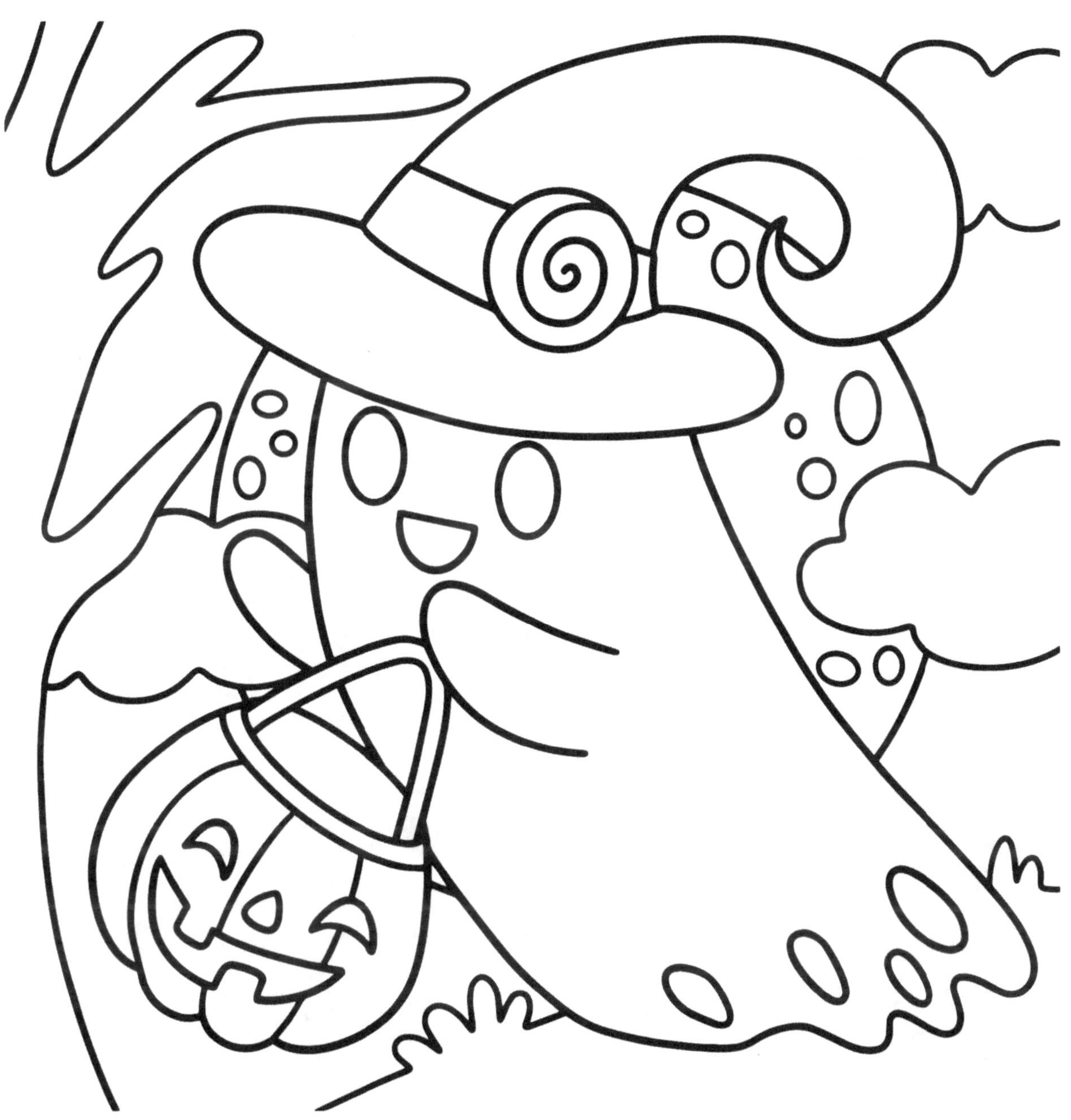

Meet the friendly ghost! It's a spooky but
kind spirit that loves to play hide and seek.

JACK THE PUMPKIN

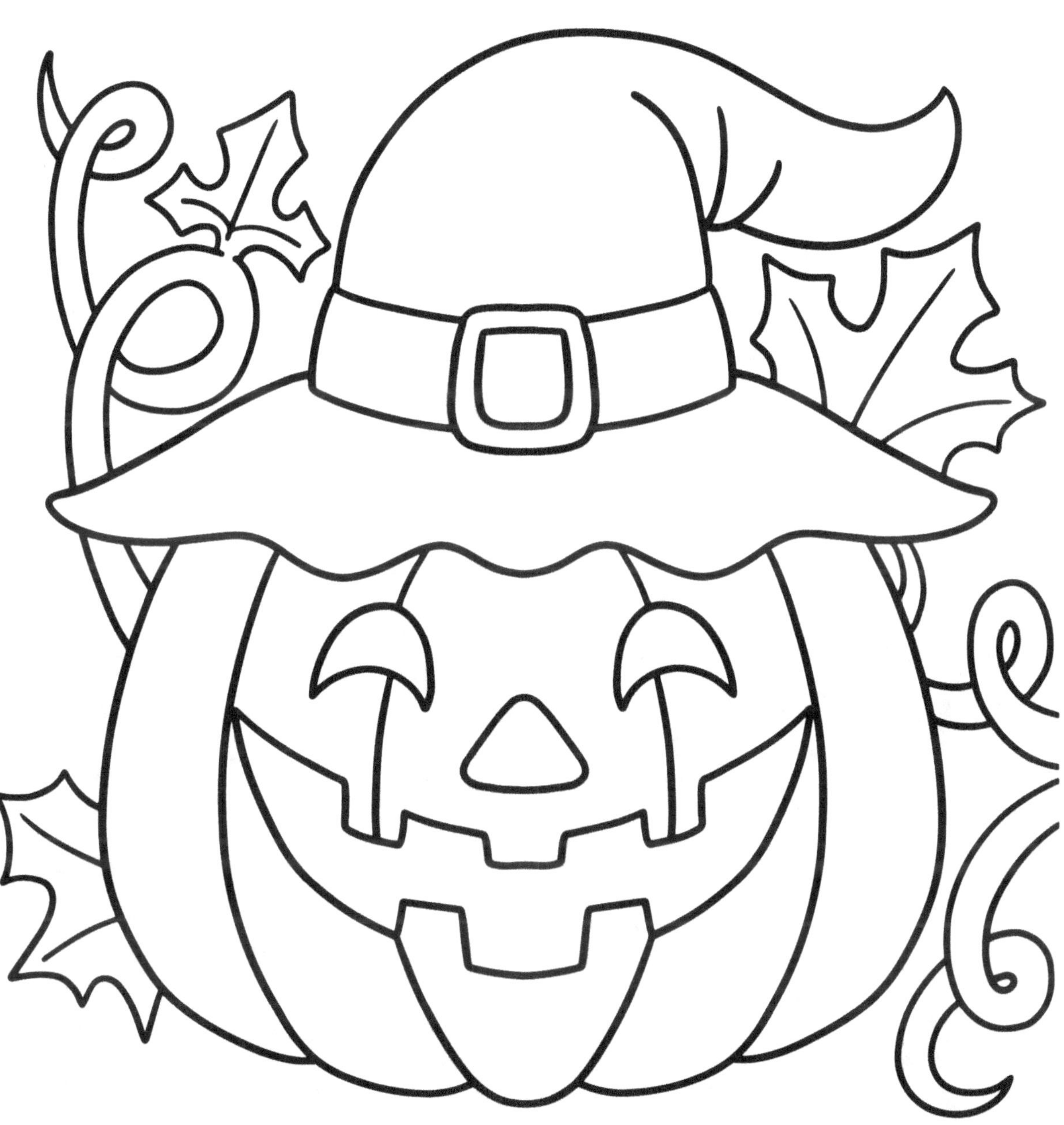

Meet Jack, the friendly pumpkin! He loves to smile and light up the night. Join him on Halloween and he'll bring joy and treats to your sight!

Which one was your favorite?

Now that you have colored every page with your vibrant colors and let your imagination soar, always remember that art lives within you. Keep exploring, creating, and filling the world with your joy and creativity. May every stroke be a reminder of how special you are and the power you have to make your world shine. Never stop coloring and dream big, little artist!

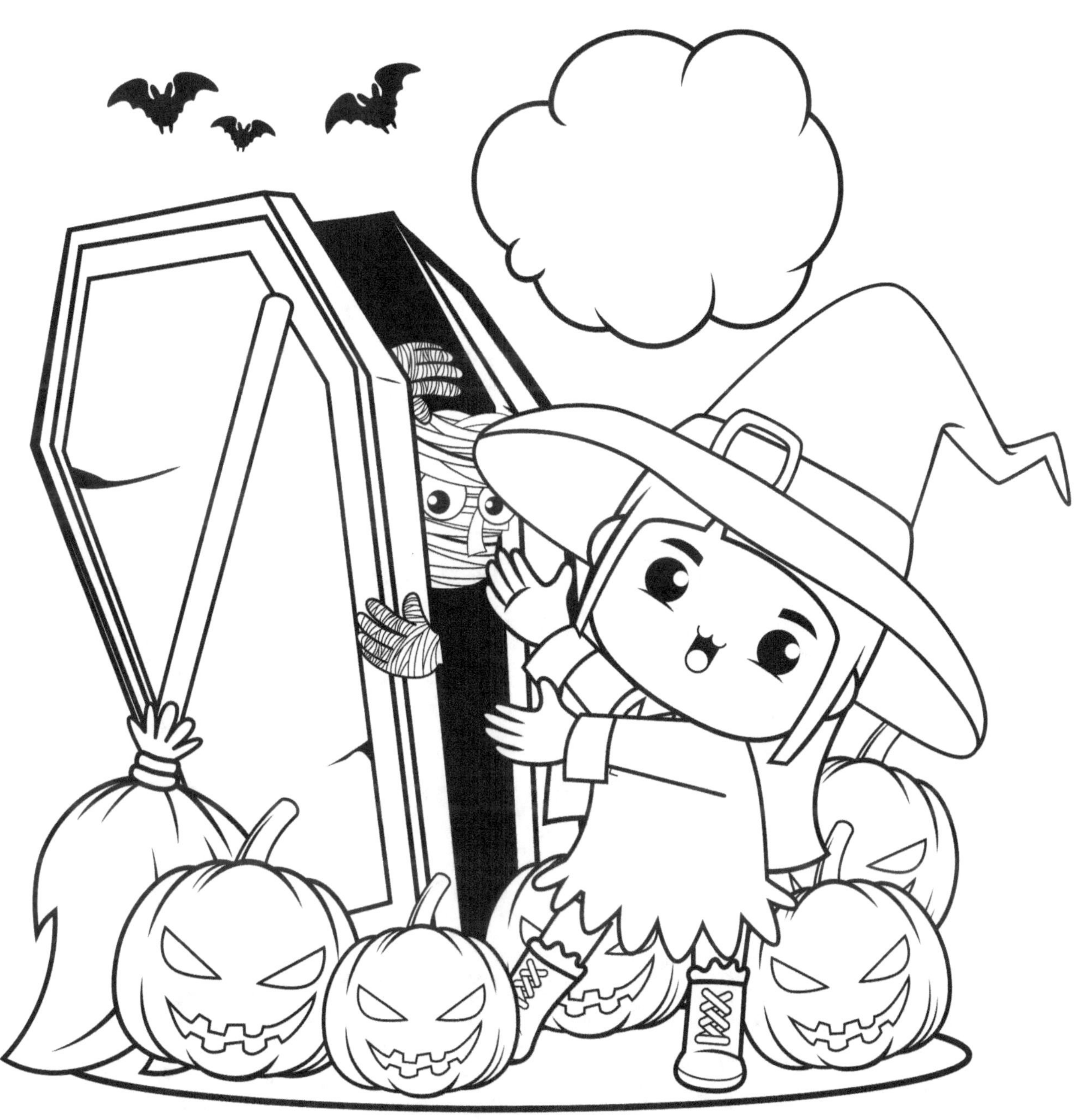

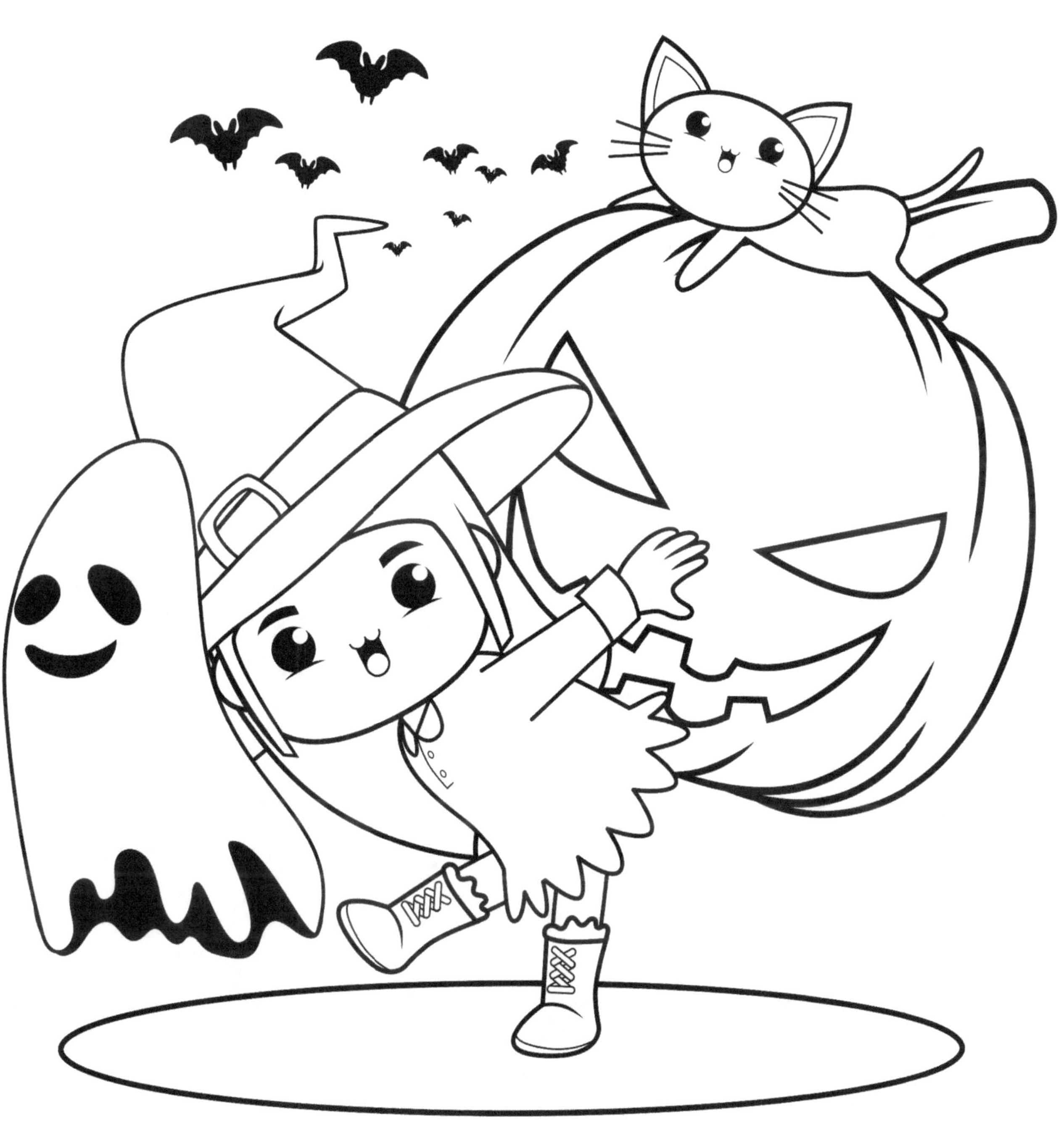

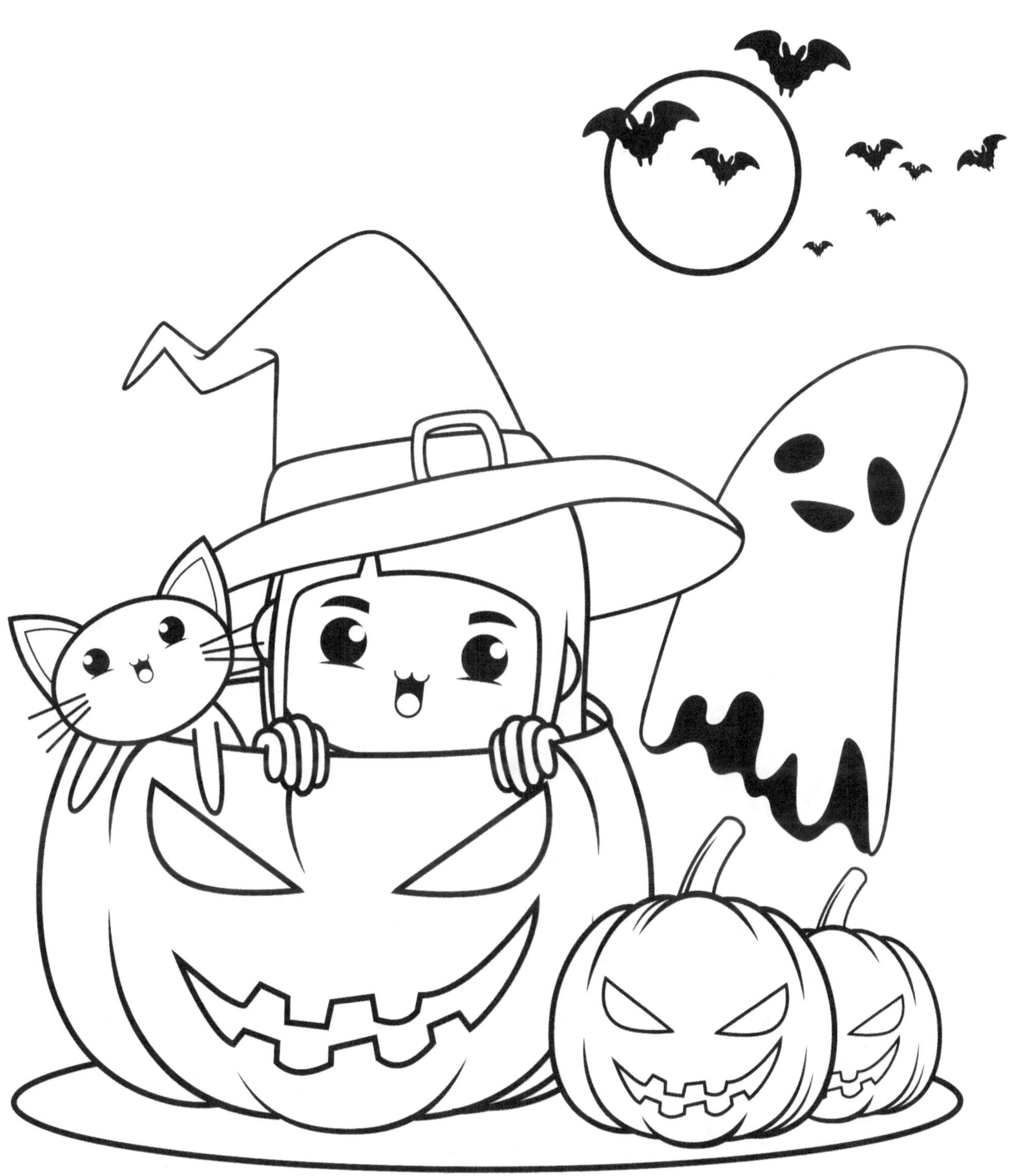

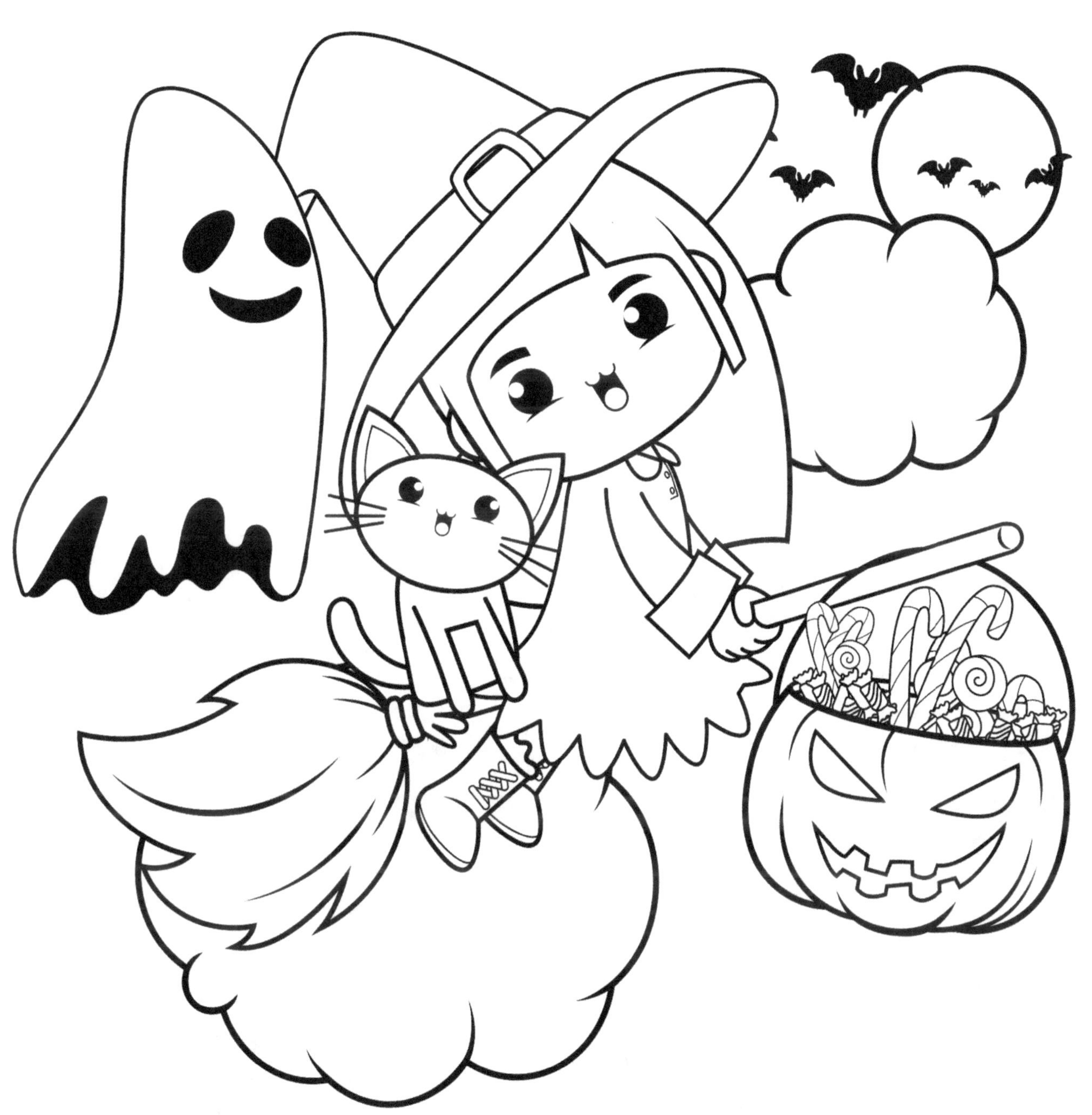

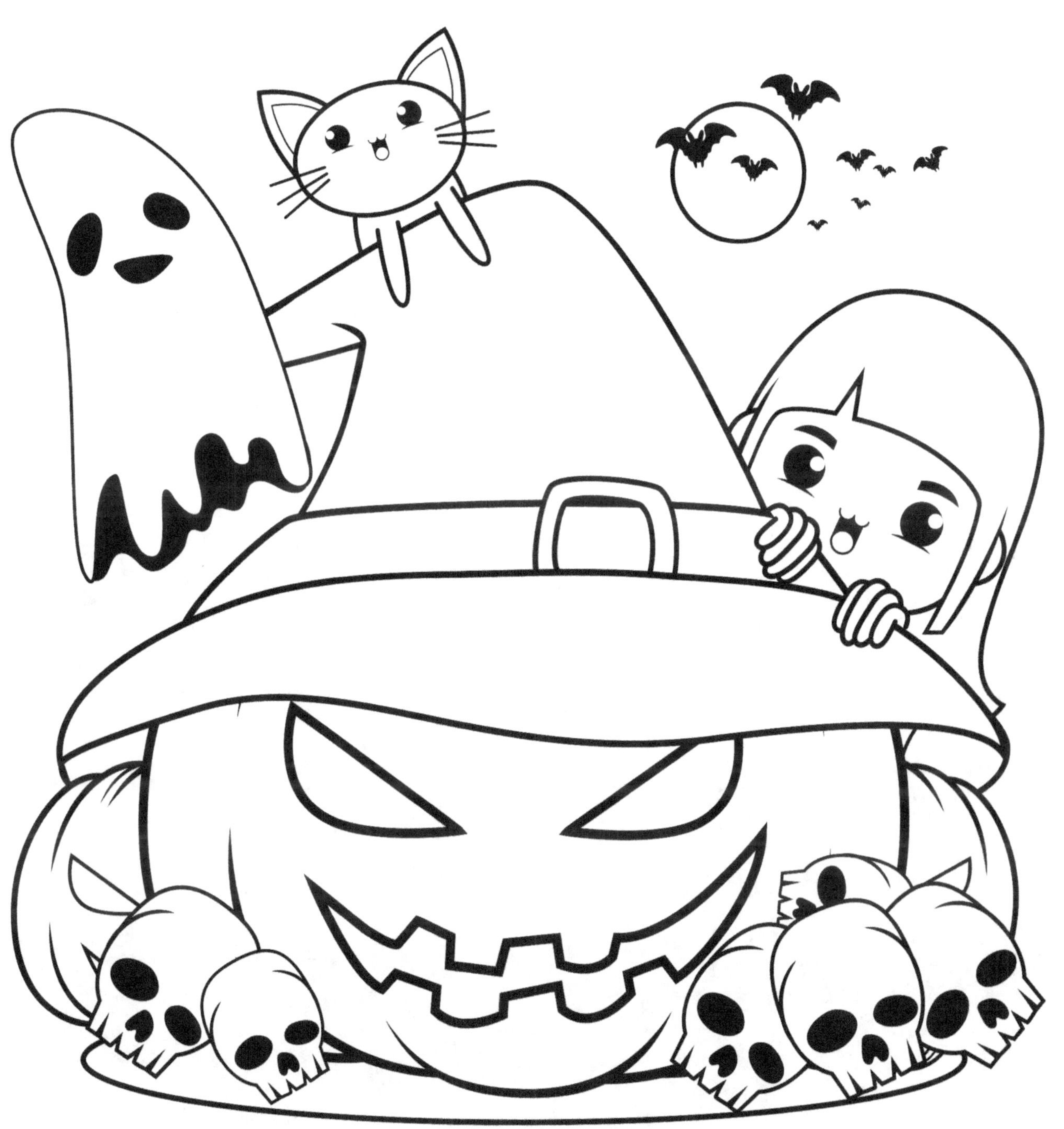

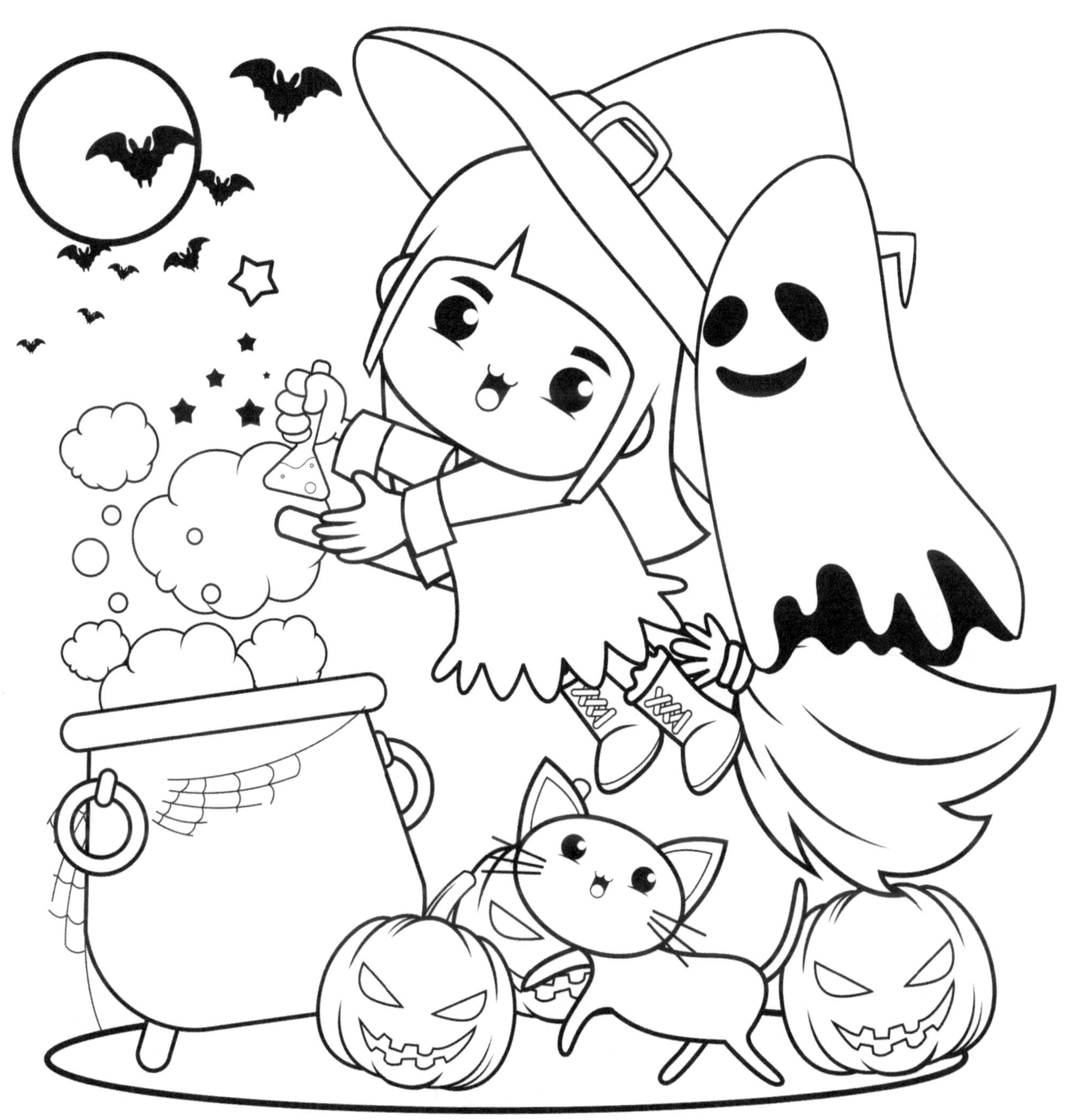

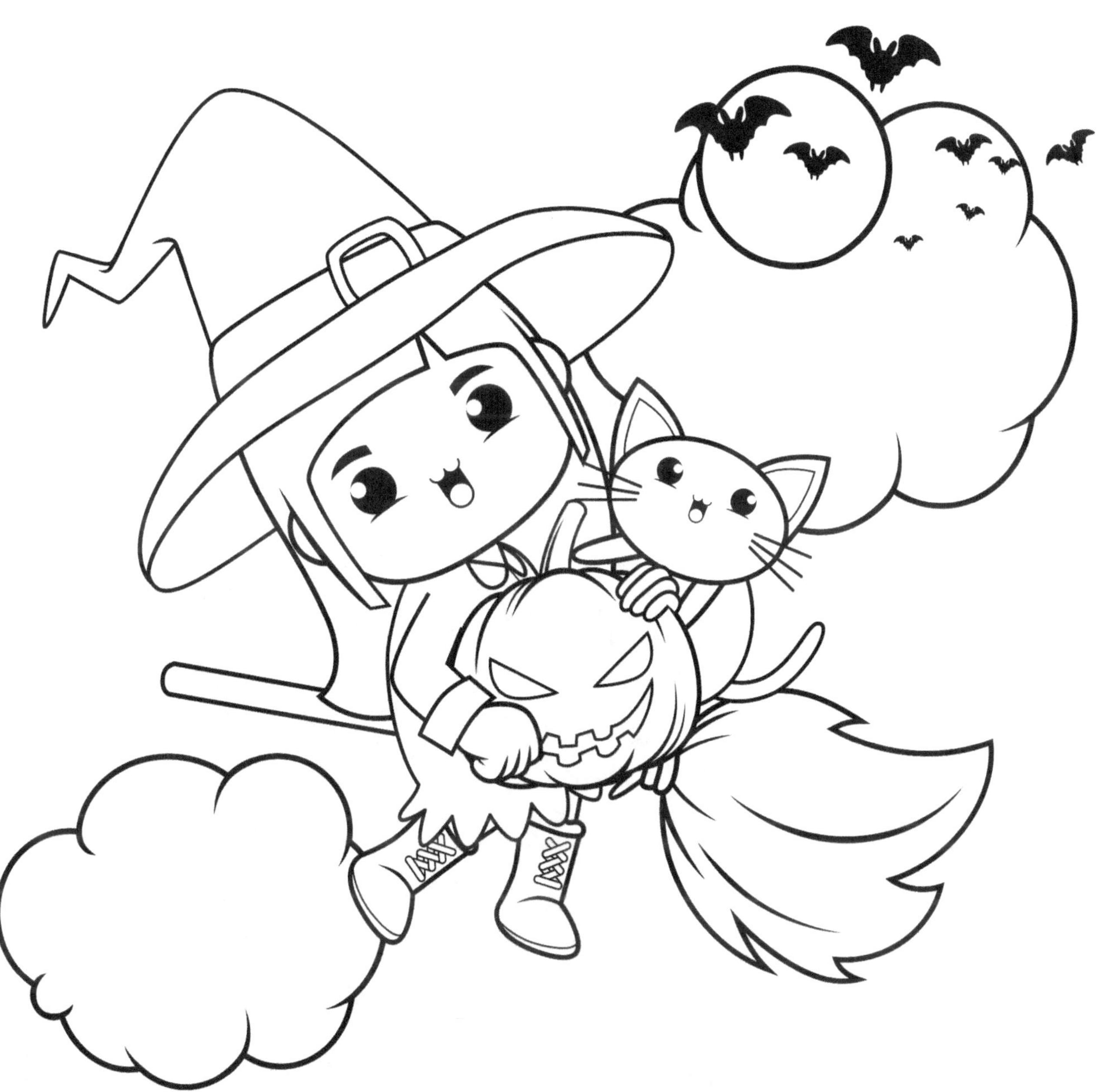

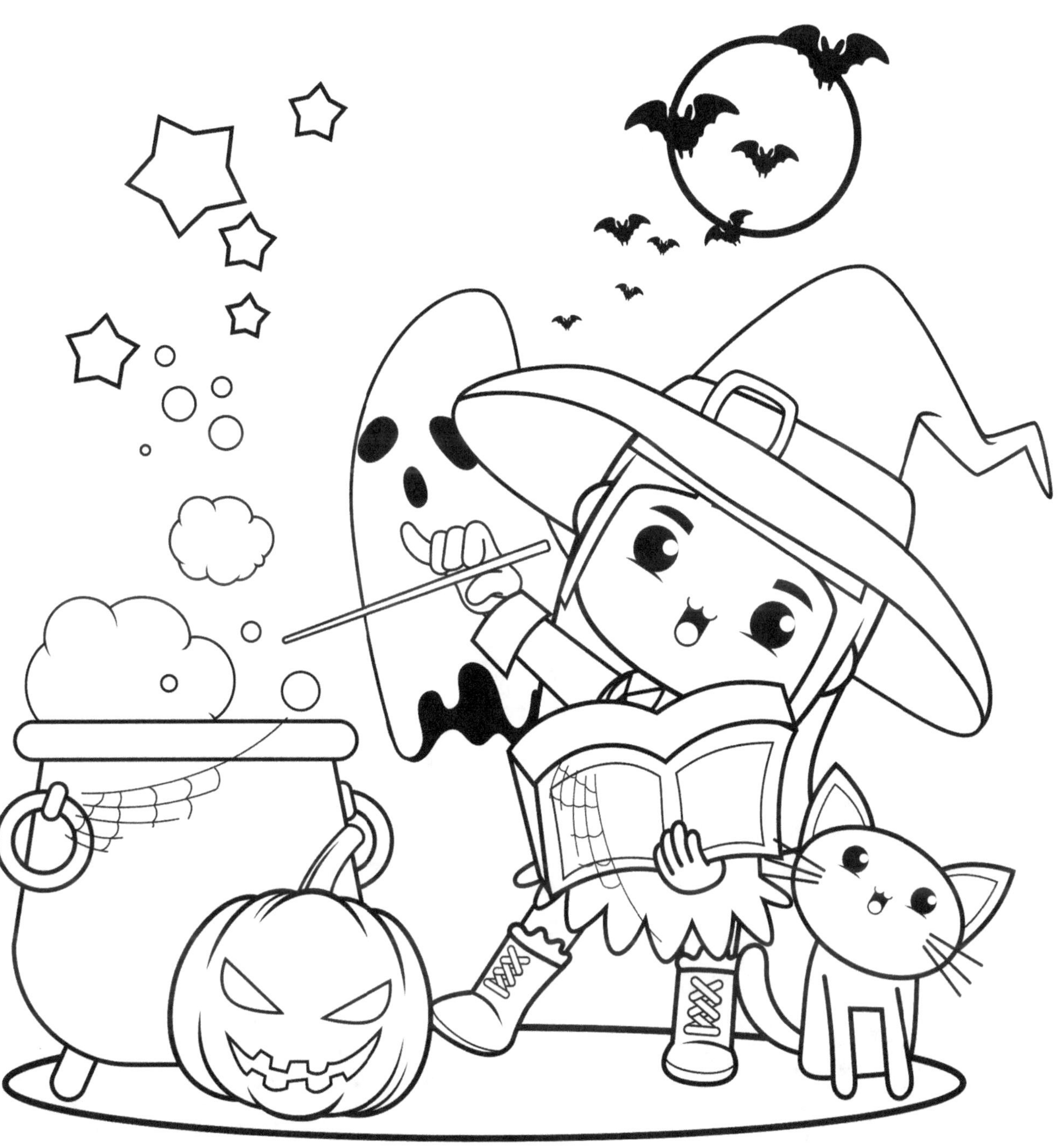

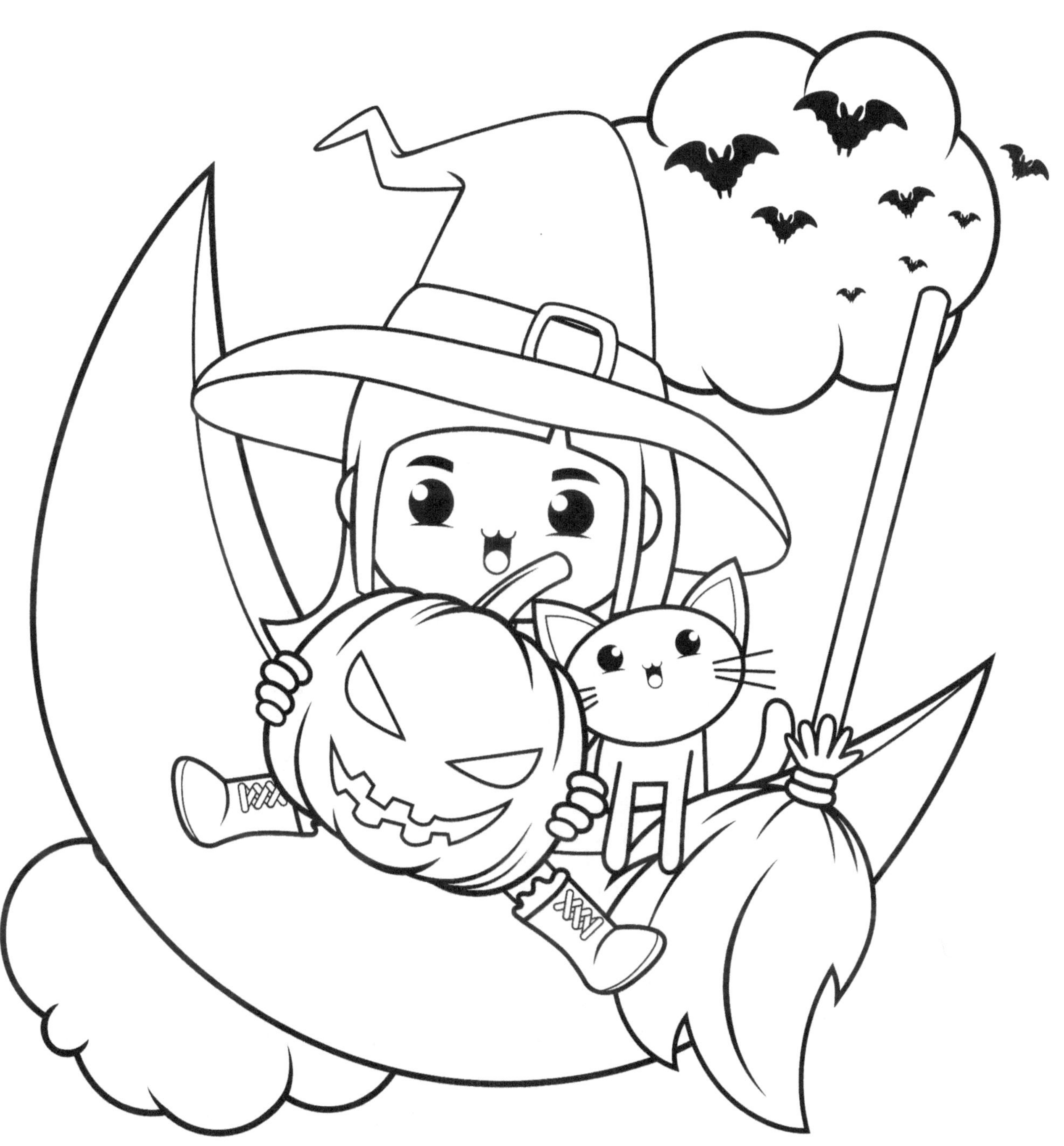

www.ingramcontent.com/pod-product-compliance
Lightning Source LLC
Chambersburg PA
CBHW080946260726
48661CB00010B/4112